YOUR KNOWLEDGE HAS VALUE

AF152057

- We will publish your bachelor's and master's thesis, essays and papers

- Your own eBook and book - sold worldwide in all relevant shops

- Earn money with each sale

Upload your text at www.GRIN.com and publish for free

Jules Miller

Marketing Information System

GRIN Verlag

Bibliografische Information der Deutschen Nationalbibliothek:

Die Deutsche Bibliothek verzeichnet diese Publikation in der Deutschen National-
bibliografie; detaillierte bibliografische Daten sind im Internet über http://dnb.d-
nb.de/ abrufbar.

Imprint:

Copyright © 2011 GRIN Verlag GmbH
Druck und Bindung: Books on Demand GmbH, Norderstedt Germany
ISBN: 978-3-656-03427-8

This book at GRIN:

http://www.grin.com/en/e-book/180610/marketing-information-system

ESSAY

MARKETING INFORMATION SYSTEM

ATLANTIC INTERNATIONAL UNIVERSITY

October 20, 2011

Marketing Information System

MARKETING INFORMATION SYSTEM

Introduction

A modern Marketing Information System (MIS) consists in managing huge amounts of data to produce meaningful and accurate information that can support managers in planning, organizing, coordinating, deciding and controlling marketing activities in an efficient and effective manner. It is more than raw data or information collected and registered whether on paper or in a computerized system for decision-making purposes. This is evidenced by the Kotler[1] who defines the Marketing Information System as "a continuing and interacting structure of people, equipment and procedures to gather, sort, analyze, evaluate, and distribute pertinent, timely and accurate information for use by marketing decision makers to improve their marketing planning, implementation and control." It is in that perspective that the current essay intends to highlight the components of a modern Marketing Information System and to explain how it provides management with valuable details concerning buyer wants, preferences and behavior.

The components of a modern Marketing Information System

The figure below highlights the components of a modern MIS, the environmental factors monitored by the system and the managerial decision-making types supported by MIS.

Figure 1 The Marketing Information Systems and its subsystems

Source: http://www.fao.org/docrep/W3241E/w3241e0a.htm

As the table above shows, there are four main components of a modern Marketing Information System. These are: Internal Report System (also

---

[1] Kotler, P., (1988) *Marketing Management: Analysis* Planning and Control, Prentice-Hall p. 102.

called "Internal Accounting System"[2]), Marketing Research System, Marketing Intelligence System and Marketing Models (also called "Analytical Marketing System").

Internal Report Systems

In general, all firms that have been in operation for a given time have some amount of information. This information is usually classified depending on its nature (e.g. financial, accounting, human resource and production and operations information). It is important for employees working in a functional department to understand how data they have in their department can help decision-makers of other departments. The latter should also appreciate how information from other departments can help them and should request it. It is in that perspective that numerous companies make available to their employees and managers some amount of internal information through intranets whereby only company's employees have access on that Web-based system. For example, instead of asking an accountant to give him/her a report on the monthly sales of a particular product, a brand management officer can retrieve that information from the organization's Intranet.

The Internal Report System has two main components: Order-to Payment Cycle and Sales Information System. The Order-to Payment Cycle describes the time it takes a company to receive and to respond orders from sales representatives, dealers and customers. Generally, consumers prefer a firm that responds quicker and more accurately than competitors. The Sales Information System deals with current and updated information on sales. It helps sales management to access valuable information about prospect and customers so as to make quick and effective feedback.

In order to provide marketing management with valuable details concerning buyer wants, preferences and behavior, some firms gather valuable information on buyer through *clickstream data analysis*. These are data generated about the number of people who visited the firm's Website and its different pages, how much time they spent on the site, what they buy and what they do not buy. That can help managers know which areas of the Website are the most visited and why so as to offer products and promotions according browsing patterns. That is very critical because customers except marketers to know not only who they are but also what they want and prefer.

---

[2]http://books.google.com.pk/books?id=KQaprS2DJvQC&pg=PA41&dq=Marketing+Information+system&as_brr=3&client=firefox-a#PPA41,M1

Marketing Research Systems

Marketing Research Systems concern proactive search of information to solve a perceived marketing problem. In general, such studies are purposeful in order to define a marketing problem or to solve a well identified marketing problem. The other forms of marketing research focus on continuously monitoring marketing environment instead of addressing a specific marketing problem. Marketing research uses both secondary and primary data. Marketing Research is opted for when it enables to make strategic decisions on the company's product, pricing, promotion or positioning; when it is the only resort for obtaining needed information for making a critical decision; when it helps in attacking the root cause of the symptoms a company is experiencing and when its result will produce significant and positive outcomes for the firm (Alex Caffarini, 2009).[3]

Marketing Research can help in avoiding bad marketing decisions. For example, Tim Hortons, a popular coffee chain in Canada opened some self-serve kiosks in Ireland but the service was a flop because cars in Ireland do not have cup holders while driving a car and holding at the same time a cup of hot coffee was very difficult. If marketing research had been conducted for that new business venture, it might have helped to notice that. Thus, through Marketing Research Systems, the customer's voice[4] can be heard and if this voice is taken into consideration in marketing decision-making, the company will likely be on the road of success. It is in that perspective that it is vital to carry out product testing and product package testing within the segment to which it is intended instead of self convincing that the product will feet buyer needs, wants and preferences. Such an approach should make a room for criticism and suggestions as well as positive feedback so as to learn buyer's wants, preferences and behavior.

However, a company should avoid 10 costly mistakes made with regards to Marketing Research, according to Alex Caffarini (2009). These are the following:
- Performing unnecessary marketing research
- Failing to establish clear purposes for conducting a marketing research
- Performing research for the wrong reasons
- Having no designated "owner" of the research effort
- Choosing the wrong marketing research vendor
- Scrimping on the research project
- Using the wrong data collection method
- Researching the wrong population

---

[3] Alex J. Caffarini, "Ten Costly Marketing Mistakes and How to Avoid Them," Analysights, LLC, http://analysights.com/Documents/10_Costly_MR_Mistakes.pdf
[4] http://www.entrepreneur.com/article/14832

Marketing Information System

- Asking the wrong questions and,
- Having no plan to act on the research results

Due to one or more of the shortcoming described above, some marketing research studies have rejected good ideas. For example, the idea of telephone answering machines was originally rejected basing on marketing research.[5]

Marketing Intelligence Systems

One of major differences between Marketing Intelligence and Marketing Research is that the latter is focused whereas the former is not. A Marketing Intelligence System is composed of procedures and data sources used by marketing managers to fetch information from the environment that they can use in making decisions. While the Internal Report Systems tell a marketing manager what happened or what is happening inside the company, Marketing Intelligence Systems help in knowing what is going on outside the firm and in getting information about the economic and business environment. Marketing Intelligence can be carried out in various ways including the following:

- *Unfocused scanning*: This is when through what he/she reads, hears or watches a marketing manager gets information that might be useful whereas in beginning he/she had neither intention nor purpose to search that information.

- Semi-focused scanning: Like in an unfocused scanning, the manager has no intention to search particular pieces of information but with the semi-focused scanning the difference is that he/she narrows the range of the media that is being scanned. He/she can for example focus on business and economic magazines and pay no attention to political or technical magazines.

- Informal search: This is when a marketing manager makes a limited and unstructured attempt to get information for a specific purpose.

- Formal search: This is when a marketing manager purposively searches information in some systematic way in order to address a specific problem. Unlike marketing research which is generally conducted by a professional researcher, formal search is carried out by a manager and the scope of the search is likely to be narrow and less intensive than in marketing research.

Ignoring collecting marketing intelligence information can have a negative impact on the success of a firm. For example, when fuel price dramatically

---

[5] http://www.web-books.com/eLibrary/NC/B0/B64/064MB64.html

increased in 2008, Southwest Airlines was prepared whereas other passenger airlines companies were not. In fact, Southwest Airlines had anticipated the problem and bought in advance fuel in large quantities for its planes before the crisis at lower prices whereas its competitors had not anticipated such a threat and purchased fuel at higher prices.

Search engines, corporate websites, publications, trade shows and associations, sales people, and customers can help in finding valuable information on buyers' wants, preferences and behavior. For example, if a firm wants to monitor what buyers are saying about it and its products, its company blog or comment areas of the corporate website and social networks like Facebook or Twitter, it can go to sites like *WhosTalkin.com*. There are other opportunities in using Websites like *WhosTalkin.com* in an innovative way whereby companies can search the blogs of people who are in their target segment and then involve them in the product or service design by taking note of their wants, preferences and behavior. In addition, publications like the *Economist*, the *Wall Street Journal, Forbes, Fortune, Business Week,* the *Financial Times, Sales and Marketing Management,* etc. are good to read to learn global business trends and consumer issues that are relevant for firms doing business in domestic and global market place. Trade shows also offer other opportunities to learn not only what the competitors are doing but also what attracts buyers to them in terms of customers' needs and wants satisfaction. But, another source of marketing intelligence concerns the firm's sales people. Let us suppose that one of the company's products is hardly bought by customers. The company would likely be inclined to talk firstly to its sales peoples to investigate on the reasons. This is because the company's sales people are like the eyes and ears of the organization. Thus, they are probably the ones who know better how the product is perceived on the market, what buyers are looking for and what competition is doing. That is why companies invest in customer relationship management systems in order to know better buyers' wants, preferences and behavior. Observing how buyers behave is another critical task for marketing intelligence so as to effectively decide how to tailor the company's offer to their wants, preferences and behavior. For example, during the latest economic crisis, many wholesalers and retailers remarked that consumers started buying smaller amounts of goods just what they needed in a week. Having notice that trend, some consumer good manufacturers managed to get their product smaller than they used to be instead of raising the prices.

Even if marketing intelligence is important as it allows marking management to know what is going on outside the company especially in the business and economic environment, illegal and unethical collection of corporate information referred to as industrial espionage should not be used by a company because it can undermine its trustworthiness.

Marketing Models

Marketing models concerns means of interpreting information so as to give direction in decision-making process[6]. They can be computerized or not. As other MIS components, they help in 3 levels of decision-making that are:

- *Strategic decision- making* which is concerned with implications involving the change of the structure of the organization
- *Control decision-making* which deals with issues related organizational policies
- *Operational decision-making* which concern the management of the firm's marketing mix.

Typical tools used by Marketing Models include the following:

- Times series sales models
- Brand switching models
- Linear programming
- Elasticity models (price, demand, income, etc)
- Regression and correlation models
- Analysis of Variance models
- Sensitivity analysis
- Discounted cash flows
- Spreadsheet what if models

Some of the tools above are stochastic whereas others are deterministic.

To illustrate how marketing models support marketing decision-making, let us suppose that a firm would like to assess the impact of advertising and sales promotion on the sales of its new powder milk product. To conduct that study, the company carries out an experimental testing in 5 geographical areas having almost similar characteristics about potential customers, brand image, consumers' wants, preferences and behavior. By the help of its internal reporting system, the firm keeps sales records for the 5 zones under study and the advertising and sales promotion expenses incurred by the company within the period under study. Let us consider sales as y_i (kept by the internal reporting system in thousand of powder milk boxes), geographical area as i and advertising and sales promotion expenses incurrent in each zone as x_i (kept by the internal reporting system in thousand of US Dollars).

---

[6] Decision-making process involves intelligence (identifying a problem), designing many possible solutions to address the problem, choosing among the alternative solutions and implementing the chosen solution.

The following table shows the data kept by internal reporting system

i	y_i	x_i
1	25	5
2	30	6
3	35	9
4	45	12
5	65	18

By the help of an analytical model called *linear regression,* the company can interpret the information using the equation of the linear slope (that is Y=a.x+b where a $=\dfrac{COV(X, Y)}{V(X)}$

and b= the mean of y minus a times the mean of x)

By using Microsoft Excel, the firm can compute linear regression.

The company can firstly compute the averages of y and x as follows:

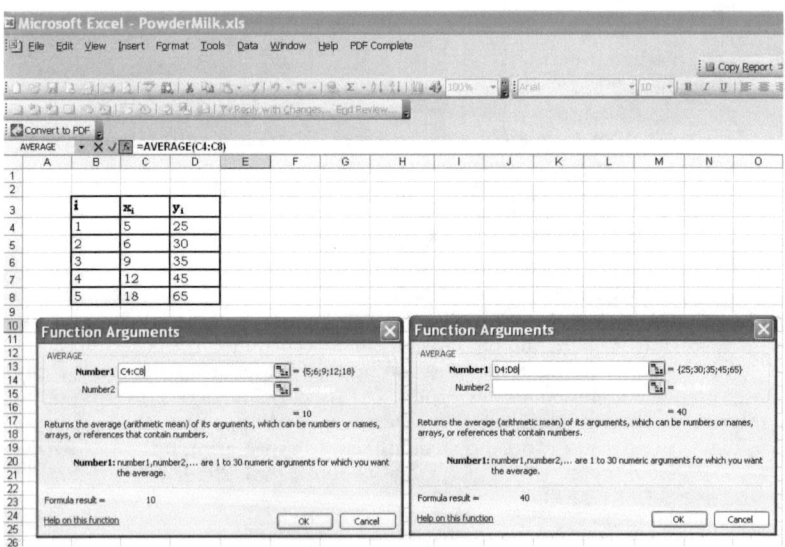

We can se that the average of x obtained through the Ms Excel formula **=AVERAGE(C4:C8)** is 10 whereas the average of y obtained through **=AVERAGE(D4:D8)** is 40. That means that the average advertising and sales promotion expenses incurred in the period under study is 10 meaning 10 thousand US Dollars whereas the average of powder milk boxes sold is 40 meaning 40 thousand boxes.

8

Ms Excel can help in computing the coefficient of the linear slope equation by using the **LINEST** function as follows:

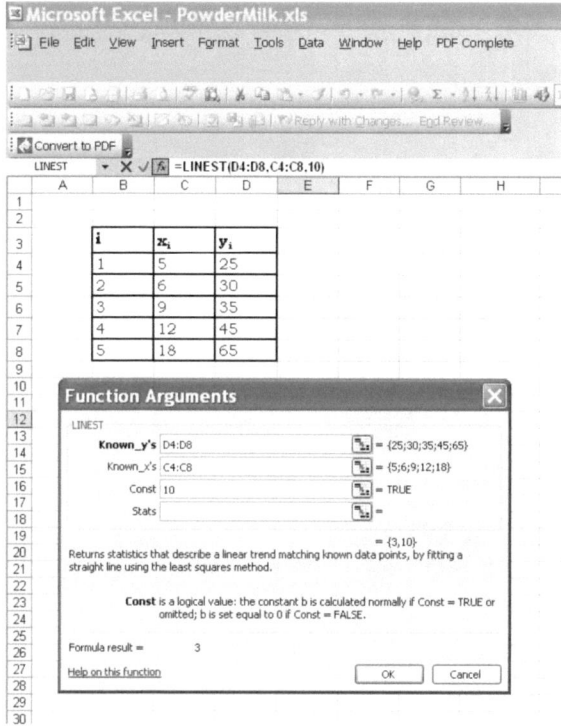

Thus, the coefficient of the linear equation called *a* is 3.

Therefore the linear slope equation is **Y=3x+10**

As the equation is found out, the company can now interpret. The equation shows that if the firm spends no thing or zero US Dollar on advertising and sales promotion (meaning that x=0), it sells 10 thousand boxes of powder milk. Since a=3, it means that one additional US Dollar (USD1) invested in advertising and sales promotion allows the company to sell 3 more boxes of milk powder.

In order to assess the quality of that linear relationship between the investment in advertising and sales promotion *correlation analysis* can be

Marketing Information System

used by the help of Ms Excel in computing the coefficient of correlation found using the **CORREL** formula as follows:

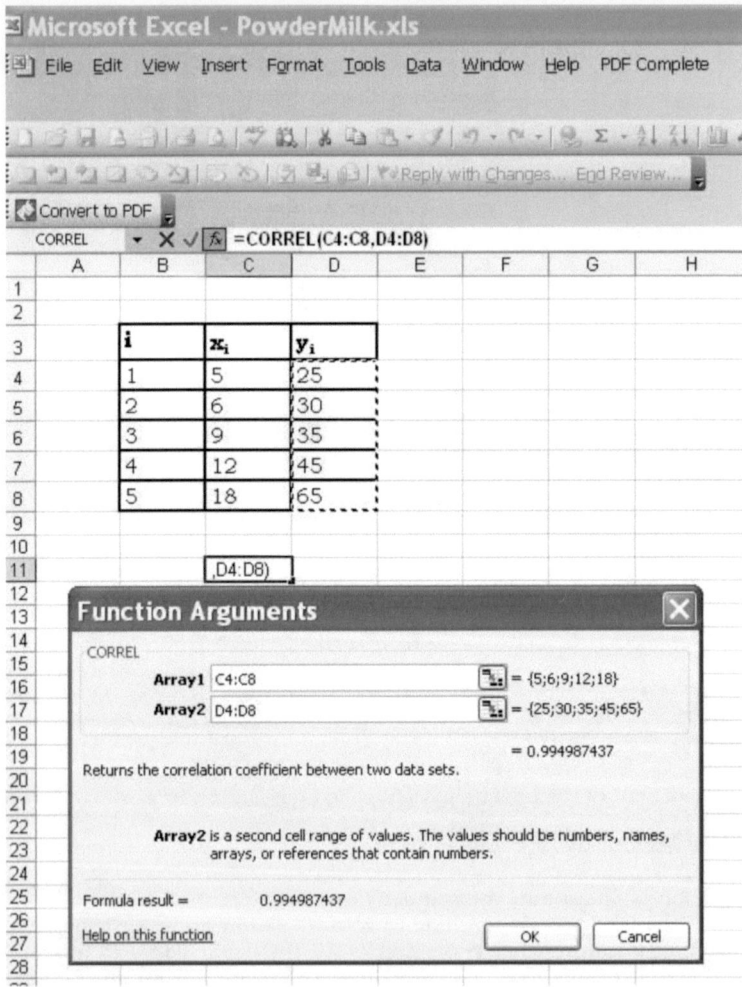

Since the correlation coefficient is 0.994987437 there is positive correlation between investment in advertising and sales promotion and sales of powder milk. Thus, there is a strong linear relationship between the two.

By the help of deterministic models namely regression and correlation tools, the company has described what happened in the experimental testing and can now use that information in forecasting. However, caution is needed while using analytical tools in forecasting. For example, for our illustration, the stability of the linear relationship or impact of advertising and sales promotion on sales would necessitate stability of the behavior of consumers and competitors and on the matching of promotion and other Ps (Product, Price and Place) with consumers' needs, wants and preferences. In addition, if the company uses the same results obtained by the help of analytical models we have used to predict what would happen if it decided to spend over 20 or 25 thousand US Dollars on advertising and sales promotion, expected results might not happen due market saturation phenomena or due to the reaction of the competitors. Therefore, caution is needed while using analytical tools in forecasting.

Conclusion

Marketing Information Systems support marketing management in strategic, control and operational decision-making. A Marketing Information System has four main components: Internal Reporting System, Marketing Research Systems, Intelligence Systems and Marketing Models. An organization should have an Internal Reporting System that allows it to gather information on its daily operations in order to find out customers' patterns to pinpoint their wants, preferences and behavior. Marketing Intelligence implies regularly collecting information so as to get to know what is going on in the economic and business environment. It can be used within the scope of ethics and legality to know consumers' thinking and perception about the company and its products or services. Marketing Models help in interpreting information to support decision making but caution is needed so as to avoid overestimation or underestimation in forecasting that can lead to bad decisions. Mathematical figures should not overshadow human behavior especially the dynamics of consumer behavior. If a company cannot answer a marketing question using its Internal Reporting System, Marketing Intelligence and Marketing Models, the last resort is Marketing Research. Unlike Marketing Intelligence which is less specific in its purposes and conducted by a manager, Marketing Research is more specific in its purposes and is conducted by marketing researchers. It can be used to hear customers' voice in regards with their wants, preferences and behavior so as allow marketing manager make adequate decisions.

References

Alex J. Caffarini, *"Ten Costly Marketing Mistakes and How to Avoid Them,"* Analysights, LLC,
http://analysights.com/Documents/10_Costly_MR_Mistakes.pdf , accessed on August 12, 2011 at 8:05 pm GMT

http://books.google.com.pk/books?id=KQaprS2DJvQC&pg=PA41&dq=Marketing+Information+system&as_brr=3&client=firefox-a#PPA41,M1, accessed on August 12, 2011 at 10:05 am GMT.

http://www.entrepreneur.com/article/14832, accessed on August 12, 2011 at 7:40 pm GMT.

http://www.fao.org/docrep/W3241E/w3241e0a.htm ,accessed on August 11, 2011 at 10:00 am GMT.

http://www.web-books.com/eLibrary/NC/B0/B64/064MB64.html, accessed on August 12, 2011 at 09:00 pm GMT.

Kotler, P., (1988) *Marketing Management: Analysis* Planning and Control, Prentice-Hall p. 102.